# THE MONSTER LIVES OF
# BOYS AND GIRLS

THE NATIONAL POETRY SERIES

The National Poetry Series was established in 1978 to ensure the publication of five poetry books annually through participating publishers. Publication is funded by the late James A. Michener, the Copernicus Society of America, Edward J. Piszek, the Lannan Foundation, the National Endowment for the Arts, and the Tiny Tiger Foundation.

2002 Competition Winners

Julie Kane (Natchitoches, Louisiana) *Rhythm & Booze*
SELECTED BY MAXINE KUMIN
PUBLISHED BY UNIVERSITY OF ILLINOIS PRESS

William Keckler (Harrisburg, Pennsylvania) *Sanskrit of the Body*
SELECTED BY MARY OLIVER
PUBLISHED BY VIKING PENGUIN

Eleni Sikelianos (Boulder, Colorado) *The Monster Lives of Boys and Girls*
SELECTED BY DIANE WARD
PUBLISHED BY GREEN INTEGER

Gabriel Spera (Los Angeles, California) *The Standing Wave*
SELECTED BY DAVE SMITH
PUBLISHED BY HARPER COLLINS

Meredith Stricker (Carmel, California) *Tenderness Shore*
SELECTED BY FRED CHAPPELL
PUBLISHED BY LOUISIANA STATE UNIVERSITY PRESS

# THE MONSTER LIVES OF BOYS AND GIRLS

Eleni Sikelianos

*Winner of the 2002 National Poetry Series*
*Selected by Diane Ward*

**GREEN INTEGER**
**KØBENHAVN & LOS ANGELES**
**2003**

GREEN INTEGER
Edited by Per Bregne
København/Los Angeles

Distributed in the United States by Consortium Book
Sales and Distribution, 1045 Westgate Drive, Suite 90
Saint Paul, Minnesota 55114-1065

(323) 857-1115 / http://www.greeninteger.com
lilycat@sbcglobal.net

This edition first published by Green Integer in 2003
10 9 8 7 6 5 4 3 2 1

Some of the poems in this volume first appeared in *Bombay Gin*,
*Cities of Chance: Experimental Poets from Brazil & the U.S.*, *Canwehaveourballback*,
*Conduit*, *Conjunctions*, *Double Room*, *Gutcult*, *Kindled Terraces: American Poets in
Greece*, *Marks*, *Mondo Greco*, *pompom*, *Puppy Flowers*, *Snout*, *Teachers & Writers
Magazine*, *Tin House*, *Washington Square*, *A.Bacus*, *The Asthmatic*, *Blue Fifth* and
*The Hat*. The author wishes to thank the publishers of these magazines and books
and Dan Featherston for printing *Summer at St- Nazaire*. She also wishes to thank
the Fulbright Foundation, La Maison des écrivians at St.Nazaire, and the National
Endowment for the Arts. Thanks also to Mary Margaret O'Hara for the use of the
title "Joy's the Aim," from her song of the same name, to Norma Cole, Diane Ward,
Clark Coolidge, Fanny Howe, Barbara Guest, and, as always, Laird.

Photograph of Eleni Sikelianos by Lisa Jarnot
Design: Per Bregne
Typography: Kim Silva

LIBRARY OF CONGRESS CATALOGING IN PUBLICATION DATA
Eleni Sikelianos
*The Monster Lives of Boys and Girls*
p. cm — Green Integer 88
ISBN: 1-931243-67-0
I. Title II. Series

Green Integer books are published for Douglas Messerli
Printed in the United States of America on acid-free paper.

*For Brenda, for Tim, & for Anne*

# THE MONSTER LIVES OF
# BOYS AND GIRLS

# Contents

*Captions for my Instruction Booklet on*
*Naturally Historical Things*

## *Captions for my Instruction Booklet on Naturally Historical Things*


All my good ideas, come
back to me!  I've done $6.00 worth
of walking today and I want you
to come home. This is not
just dream-jargon. The city is out there, and you
are a citizen—What's
your report?  I want the animals
to come to me from far and wide
over the frightened grass, just as they would if
this were a wishing-apple and the mountains
were hollowed by shadow. What do you want?  A cup of
shit on the subway?  (I saw it)  Light
flashing out from behind
the elevator.  Details
to make a philosophy?  These won't.

But I will shout this dream out to you
as soon as I have learned another bird-bone by heart

bird, daughter of my own body, the fragments of its royal
    head floating up, occipital;
Late summer wears an eerie light
on utility poles & shows
the creatures we moved through to get here:
        reptile, raven

        varied faces emerging
        from the
        totem


Flocks of limbs come dark & forward, wings drawn down
    one by one

        This is a subregister of a larger field, perhaps
        of a desert hunt with wild dogs


I suspect our city
will soon be laid to ashes
Our island city
Rowing out over the river in the dark
They have divided
geometry onto it, stripped
off the mosses, stripped off the rocks, and replaced them

with concrete blocks. When you are thinking
    in the dark, think
of our city

as stitched dynamos switched on & shining at midnight,
    a vast land
of electrically charged siding and craters, & over it we lay
in the bright & in the dark if you fill your brain
with Boston or New York

in this our talking America we will reach
Thales by water
Bangor by sea
Anaximander by air
a large iron gate

Take Paris by river
Anaxagoras by thought
Take Zoraster by fire, Jesus
and the mutts by love,
Take fire by flashlight, take flight, between the allegory
    of each
is a narrow equatorial belt where everything is
    angular and real

## *Heaven*

What was it I saw at the top
of the world as I fell
asleep last night?

Cats arguing on the rough roof

The instant those fiery lilies let go
a handful of flame petals dropped
to the kitchen floor  & the men & the women begin

the war of the orchids
The land of politeness inside my head said

you occult deep notion of nothing
you average spiritual manhood you
sachems of molasses, you hidden national will
you fractals, splintering powwows of disorder
you ladder in the meadow
up which I climb in pointed shoes

Listen:

There is a great lake called Pleasure
the color of your eyes and nestled
in the bay—

Out of black rock:
a fresh-water trickle

### Joy's the Aim

I am thinking
of holding the sleeping bus rider's head in the dark,
    it's a weakness

skimmering at the surface
waters, bodies'

shimmering liquids, a leaky
oil can.  If you can find the ditch anywhere,

same sand pile pitched forward out of earth, proto-
industrial works, valves
of the heart, some stranger's creaking
elbow's angling into my path, come

follow that bone, my beacon,
frame, rest stop, house, reflecting
the whole body aflame for when
we stop to rest together and I think up a world
    made bright by

what, my love?  Words
were the brightest world, I wanted
to say, but perhaps the world
is brighter still—the white

cobbled stones that lead down
to the station lying in light, dumb
and alive, and you lie there, too,

the green & yellow figs tongue-tied in the light
on the round table, their interior life
tense with sex, wise

pearled seeds in pink that think up a world
made bright, no words.  In the age of tall ships careening

the small island harbor named Madame or Man
will excavate the watery site
below skin or thighs to indicate
where smiles have been. I find myself a casual

organism, sex
made sad, corn's false smut in a teary morning light—
    a shredded

veil of golden tones scrambling to reassemble the sweeter
    hours, stashing
pistachios in my armpits. A hair snaps

between me & observation—Shut

my eye to the planet
to assemble a dimensional map of roving
bodies from my radar mast—43.5 million square miles

of Earth covered over
with humans and parts. All our world's particles

are looking at each other in that thing
called space. Before quantum fuzziness gives
way to tangible bodies the moon
smears across skies. Let me

hold you You universe world you, all our possible
    irresponsible histories hovering
together like lovers in super pretzel-positions
of elbows, limbs, particles that penetrate all my stuff. There
    is a discrepancy

in this macroscope, lift up the skirts. Around me a frayed

         and fancy they
wear unbearable situations on their sleeves, sorting
through receipts, writing thank you notes, snapping bullets
      into place—


cuff links or curve feelers? I do, I do feel this gentling bend,
      can you
hand it over to me? Walk sweet & drift toward borders
to nudge apart my states & spin


into the technique of the working river
sifting waters, riddling,
liberally quitting Earth; bird; not like that swallow
but a metal bird, a plane I saw change
energy at higher elevations near the breach then glide
below clouds like floats of ice & loose
itself in sky.
         May birds that mount
be highest, fly
swift, have a wing more sturdy, material more
flammable for exploding blue than those
forty horses marked Mystery & acquiesce   teethed
      & tearing—
I can barely taste the quiet for all the noisy purrings
my bodily motors make.

### *What I know about the world that is evil*


When the dark tail began loosening the lake
came forth a chiton in the shape of a kite
and "the tiny bottle of Mars Black that you hold in your
    hand" begins to write
our history now, all the high
velocity / low velocity  movements
with a light touch upon dark things

    Dark to fit the times
    Light to light

the trees' shadows pressed into the ground, fingering it  Filter
your own leaf pattern over hillsides, suburbs
stitched up like snails nautilus-shaped
Huge spidery forms arise in the land, dust-born
creeks flash out, pencil-thin blades run coppery  We grow
waterless and move
       a new wing for

                stay, happiness
                fly, happiness

Break the lake
where the unborn lights of many kinds begin to be
your tiny birds your tiny kind

### The Cooking Stove Has a Thought

The crystal dials shift
    in the liquid brain when it gets
off the subway—
      A whole hemisphere's twilight's twisted
        itself back to shadow where a yellow idea rises.
    The sun
comes, its dark
  thinking eating at a center knot, its something-crystal
                 lights a pilot or a thought.

          The cooking stove has a thought
          inside it, a blue flame like a flickering
          stone at the dark mouth of the burner

          If only I could have as many
          thoughts as stoves
          of stones—


      If you tap the finger
    on a brain it will burn
        the finger, brain—it will

turn left or to the right when
    exiting the subway.
            Have you been the noisy neighbor
who disturbs your neighbor's sleep?  Have you written
a musical description of having your gall bladder
    removed?  Mostly
        humans are the same.  Some build mean

        hybrid half-lynxes, others, some
            city with columns.


Someone lift us, let
some fool written-for-written come up slow; let

k's and g's collide when things get
too near my thinking, a ricochet in the inner
ear where dark thoughts are accruing
through the things things think


The guileless grass is sutured still
Salmon built from lace arise from quiet lakes
The swans carrying winter on the wing are

our ideas

of beauty expanded as the pack-ice splinters
to include a woman with a blown-out face, lost her face
in accident or age  Worry
& thinking carved
it, she wears
no picture of a previous self pinned to her sleeve. It's
you, when we were all small
      & the sides of the city
were lit up around the heart
of the river like a carnival, & *that*
was beautiful.


Or hulking men, black, brown or white, who
    go to movies by themselves and cry
    when plots twist
    the loose limbs of children into stars in
    sunny play-yards. Yes, those green
    whiskers *are* the trees, each leaf
    threatening to melt itself
    back up
    toward the sky if

    you look through it with
    your eyes

Real math shimmeringly swimming somewhere
on a plane high
above the head—Nothing

ever came from heaven, not even
your foul
mouth, child, unleashing
Alice Cooper's brutal planet—Does he know the
military method
of taking an M-16 apart?

An internal object rises
as substitute to the missing
world-parts,

chaos, heavens agape, open
space, as poured
from a honey jar; chaos, moreover, an open
principle devoid of god-like attributes

Howfore, for example, of these the waves
that resembled the heart, the night-

bones, mares of *frantica* where the mind
wanders through a landscape without fur, but with fear, or

over the beach, the black waves
lapping high-high up
& wets our stuff. I was lying there
in the sandy cove, ready

to clamber farther back, the black
waves sink into the stiff sand their dark
trash… … I scramble up the cliff to look down
into the rumbling bay where horses begin
   to fright & shoot
out of corrals, straight
into the royal
crystal
blue, across
the ocean bottom, galloping
along the furrows of the sandy bed, beneath the water;
   & me, & you

whoever you are—shooting at them as in old
movies when a horse is lame, & the thundering booms
till the underwater pier rises and writhes
to shake itself free, splintering

off to drift away, dark
spirit of the water. Will I fail

in a brittle manner, like glass, or will I fail
in a ductile manner, like gold? The cult of frosty
scores discarded in the river will soon be lit
   again. Some yeoman
with a dent in his side is calling me back
through the airwaves whence I
wandered, where I dreamed I dreamed
a floating hoarfrost thought woven
dense & tight over human skin

### *Footnote to the Lambs*

1. You shall hope to know the power of the imagination
2. You shall wish to be intellectual, be somebody; you shall
   forget about bombs
3. You shall dream of a caravan circling lush trees
   & live in dirt balls, with no sugar, no swaying allowed
4. You, loveliness in your Grecian tires, good citizens
   of sheepdom, smoking hashish, hush
5. You shall come from the Azure

# *Melospiza melodia, Mon livre d'oiseau*

In this landscape:

scattered stations from which a pair or pairs of eyes
    might observe

the scorpion's "bright hooks"
silhouettes of migrating birds against the moon; a field
    where land-
scapes diverge; winter's closing of lakes coming
    on, and birds

between their breeding regions.   Between the hills, a
    confluence, crumbling

                      The Grey-cheeked Thrush
      takes off

from home to head
toward other homes. Something distills, heavy
industry;  hinted-at
hit and runs untangling,  hawking questions of the soul's

defunct & tabulating high

TV-tower corpses; unravel this guttural; our capacities
    to home
at different elevations and hours of the night; cars speeding
pleasure at our heels, our shoulders

invented in curves, birthmarks
lit up

## *Letter to self*

Souciant
self, something was keeping me
from crazy, but I don't know
what it is.  Could it be

when I slipped East
to a city that winds up around us
meandering a park to put in my urban
pocket, a petite
tangle of green?  Here is my homeland. Where?
where is it? In a ball of verdant string
that leads leafy

to the night that great hero Hector was played
by a poodle in our public gardens and I made

a life's thought on love
night by night, when love was in the land
of heaven's prototype      where corrosives revealed

what truth was hid
in hell.      When our loves are laid

in unorganized sleep in lands
far away      we will awake up & want
to wedge a ladder into what
is iniquitous in us; softer
tissues wear
grooves of history
into bone;   What we get
wrong we do not notice but
what others do

        The mountains, silent blue
crabs, backs hard and humped, inching
back to sea—the primal features
of those founding creatures
who lie buried in us, my city, my land,

my love
I came here to kick your ass
but did I I believe I did kiss it instead  Quick

the division between energy
& thought will
soon fall away

## *Shadows of a Gazetteer*

What is this city in which we sit here?

The smooth plausible green
Ruins of this town or that

To inquire of the stones & fields & compile: What
   are your thoughts
  on history, what happens
    after death?

      After death, you will feel gravity in each tiny muscle
      of the face move more precisely, hear

      Neanderthals playing through bone-pipes

      powder blasts of snow, ice like a lead glove thieving
      over trees

      You will arise, go to Ninevah
      (she goes West instead, to Tarshish)

If you find anything, you will find everything, thus
    it follows
you will find everyone

not the dream with the devils in it
not the dark Armageddon

but the dream of the ancient walled city in the
    sloping dark
a red paper garland strung about the place to look
    like poppies feathering in the breeze—

the most delicate constructions, like bubbles—
    They are poems.  Know
the most deliciousest honeyishness;

the black stars over Lakonia;
the quick liquefaction of cats in the night;

life, life in its accessories & motives; music
& gymnastics that render it
    smoothish.  Before death

mind lies in the lap

of the dabbling heart, it is a doubling

of heat
touching life at a tangent

Man lies in the lap, woman, of an immense volcanic
   harbor tonight.

## First Greek Poem

I the roses love in the garden of Adonis
I the salted fry of marguerite love, the one chamomile, the
    tiny white that snaps
        dancing in the gutter with funny
I reddest poppy painted in blood love
Love I the final columned crown
Ever a flower inventory wept, I dreamt
Of death, wedding flower; treading
        purple will I go
Into that drowning house
With wet little lambs one-day old *(arnakia),* white horses
    *(waves)* lapping
        at the heart-knobs
When the slave pumped the handle, and the water rose

## *Sleep, Sleepwalker*

Sleep,  sleepwalker

on a small half-earth found in a world
   of floating
      fluid gold

I think it strange
   to fly over the sea—
& see there the little whirlpools of thought
   streaking across the water—

   the imaginative imagines it made
   the rivers & beasts & sea

& all the Animal forms of wisdom
(mathematics, instinct)

The female, pale, dark & dense

depicts the hardened crust
that protects the material universe
& all its fallen dimensions

our state in soft mention
clothed in penultimate night

when the lineaments of the human form
are revised     in sleep


Everywhere we go the earth keeps
        tight trees, loose
      houses, blue
lights flickering on the Washington Bridge

& little bones housed in the seahorse's skull

Vulgar fish
        in a father's pouch
      the embryo has no mouth

with which to say
of tiny ghost horses floating transparent, hippocampic


By artificially slowing the heart
we can see
the stoned cherry at its wobbled pitch, independent
    sun rays of a
seahorse's fin, go to seahorse
heaven, a sea house to which
      we spin 3 x 3



When the Cuyahoga River burst
into flames, our
ancestors never dreamed
the face of the Earth
blanketed brown over the broken
shore choked with us

      The same smile
            as the world's smile?
      The cracked face
            of the Earth?

& so our animals weave
a small success at the edges
    red fox, horned beetle

Razor wire around the garden
of Eden, I'm seeing all the seeded lakes
from the air, seeking

    air-borne hairs, a soul's detritus

This is a snake-free environment,
sneak-free, but poison blazing is our secret

The Falls curve around
the collar bone of Niagara

the sun withdraws its hand
to caress a lazy smile riding
weathered lips up
toward a stunned star

What have I chosen for the shape
of my epiphany?—

Was it this

river, this

republican,
this,
the white soft gift
of the sheep?

This eidolon of my wild
career as a ghost's ghost, one shade
down there around Hercules' knees, one up here striding

under clicking leaves

Of all the let-go secrets
of all the wild beasts-world below

birds first
in my horizontal gesture
of sound to regesticulate the world once-prisoner-
to-world-view back to pure sound    Let's
make a vertical noise
above the lakes, attach it

to an (unknown) unowned
object—Is there still one
left in the world?


Planes like black
& silver gnats
slide down
the sky—oh
that so sucks

when the shining cars like ducks are slicking up & getting
    snared
in trees

The river is out there sliding
to our right in the darkened
even—we don't have to see it this
Friday night to feel its
sweaty cogitation like
a caterpillar slinking along on its
watery arms & legs

We are stuck at a spot along the tracks waiting
for another train trucking

the opposite
way from us
to pass—Here, there are only
single-tracks so can I seem

to slip my mind
from its lazy path or back
to descriptions of delicate
blue the mind might have
received?

What is your river thinking?

Silent thoughts of cars
creeping across bridges,
a dark pressure on the tired café-colored
creatures fiddling in mud-bed muck

All our fingers work in this world,
which is good for getting
our hair tied back into rubber bands, & helping us reach
the Bronx, if that's
where you want to go.

Shake the world's dust from your
      feet, William
Blake

feel the furnace
of a genuine quince-shaped storm,
dark & scratchy like the one
on the dream horizon

            I want to go to the elevator
& ascend in the cool
wind that lifts us
in our just-awake traits
into the dusk, & our skirts asking questions

of cringing atoms singing like brass bands in the closet

I will make the music for you, a view
with no pictorial illusion of volumetric space

Because how many Saturdays have you wasted
smashing up the mall, tangling
on the briny edge of corpus bones?

Let the west wind
asleep on the lake
leap on the lake

Little drawers of night
demons laugh, the unpredictability of
a negligee
roughed up
by time

### *I Will Not Go to Space*

I will not go to space
in your rusty rocket "that rests
on coral waves" deeply
deeply golden in the frangible glass

Golden, you kill me
with your little mungo things, in the "Is he
dead yet?" game.  For us humans, it's real
when a cat interprets that dad's death. That cat
doesn't know we're not married, nor
what we are, shiny beads for eyes, little qua qua
of the ordinary legs
of ordinary women, and the men
who love them, them
ordinary legs, and the women who do

Golden, five million flowers' worth per pint
of honey to the left or to the right
of the sun; the translucent white gloves
of ghosts of larval bees tell the story
of an idling memory of a friend's house

in flames. We extinguish it. But when the soul's
afire, add kindling. But, golden,
break my glasses, sip this folding golden
whiskey, let the talkies
of Kevin Costner get blurry in our minds, tan-colored
    pretzels battling
over the batter's stand as the sun sets over the West
and Western clouds on
Dog's Neck, nothing prepares us for death.

## The Monster Lives of Boys & Girls

*omni omni homonym*
*omni humanym*
*omni anima*
*omni immortalis*
*omni rushtophil & rushing*
*omni rushmore*
*omni rustabus*
*omni manatee & mandible*
*omni omnibus*, tell me

am I the daughter of a city
or am I the daughter
of a man?

This urban wrapped rose, dog rose wrapped
in particulate air, where flies

an urban bumble bee and all, and the female sparrow, adept
at aphid picking, comes to feed amidst delphinium on
     Avenue B

            Ho, sparrows, knocking the petals
off flowers, leaves
            off trees, tell

how to display
the monster lives of boys & girls
strutting in finery down Avenue A

Boy: born half lion half dirt
Girl: born half glittering steel half hayseed
Both: Half Nantucket Nectar half shit
            half genial dumb-wit

A skyscraper with an arm
and half a huge neck budding out
                    The architected hand grabs
at air    but there is no
brain there    to instruct it
what to do
        What to do?
                    Ho! hummingbird human hybrid building

female/male will melt away or be made
more ornery as concerns grow about

how my mind grows out
of the side of the City    how
my self takes the shape
of the Chrysler    and I am thus pointed &
gleaming in afternoon heat, spliced
    with the sound of the crosstown bus (M15), the

wild dog variety of
people around.  Birds in New York
are growing big consciousnesses now
all the sparrows are growing
self-conscious & telepathic, empathic radar sound
waves ripple forth
from all starved starlings' skulls, the mistaken telemetry
of the Bronx Zoo is messing us
up.  Something is missing this morning.

        Seriously tone deaf subway cars
        are my private communication
        with the screeching of wheels

My voice is coming back to me, it's
cities laid over
the catalog of vanishing systems

All the kids are begging with my voice-over
all the moms & dads for something, since it's
Saturday, June.

Daddy, look, it's a Spiderman butt, please please
I want it!  I really want

that shiny micronaut bubblegum wrapper, everything!
like an expense account at the Ponce de Leon Federal Reserve
full of sun & heat & multiplex personalities
and for you to be here with us, alive and living in the hot heat
of a musically inclined Brooklyn street ribboned out like
"pretty silky black songs" & honeycomb, with a bottle of
    cold gingerale in my hands


As you know, I'm writing this for you and you only, mutant,
all these little details I put in for you—this man
sweating in blue stockings & red leotard suit, he's got it
backwards, that grid of this world
that shows the mute web of human endeavor   kissing
animals & plants

This word, the word "hierarchy"

the word "summer"
summer summer summer thunder, thief,
thief, thief in the night it's something
you love, it's here
only for you

### Pool Poem
*(for Isabelle's pools)*


There might be a blue eye of a pool
where you arrive in pitch
at the edge eroding night   diatomaceous birds
exploding how their lightly plying air

Do I own the word Tendons now I think I do   Still
Asshole is for girls
Bitch is for boys

Bonnie & Clyde arrive
at the edge, their dresses felicitous,
a fiery distance. The task of this corset,
you of your tight sideboards, people,
and the pictures of people
related to you dying to ride

time, penetrates
the slabs lining
the sidings of pools—an ocean
reliquary asleep under the breach

of a jacaranda tree; tortillerias brought deckside
spin out bullet-like bright curves of sunshine & I will
frontyard this luxuriate thought of the eye in the whole of
    the decaying face, driving
through a world weighted down in dirt, limbs water-
    bewitched


Now I see
flesh was supposed to be air
        or at most smoke
        If smoke, let it
light & move over a city turning on & off at dusk

Hire a construction crew to renovate
the crumbling space in that dream

In that dream, "thought my name a Rock" at
beach side, high tide, with crisis forms to fill out, as crisis
    forms along the ice
hyenas sleep underwater in tidepools closed off by rocks
and tiny ouds like gods go

  grr

the rooftop of ruining beauty
set down in weeds

## *A Carnet for the Loved Love*

Does or does
not an event
have a position
in space?  Here
is an event:
My loved
love is splashing
his/her toes in the
water.

His toe-
nails grow

greedy.  In the somber & emotionally
repressed environment of
enfin-de-siècle America, does
or does it not
have to do with
craters
aethers
that blue

shirt blue
cap of that
kind of beer, bus
transfer,
shade, crack-
pipe, Naltraxin & oh
shade, that
Turquoise
Lodge sleigh
ride shade thing.  Light
might not be able to turn the corner

of the street, but my loved
love turns
corners on more streets than I
can keep track of.  Just as they were trying to set a limit
    (boundary)
to light, my loved love turns again.  But
if I name light, like looking
at a direct light (sun) I also name pain.  At the happy
    appearance of color, if I put light
at the back of his knees, he will dream.  These are lights
    from lamps and
maps and elsewhere.

All the

beauty of all the
light
blue finds itself in
Eu-

clid.  Is it my love or light that gives
from black to white?  The dark is rough, the light
is smooth, but the weight of light is like

with ants.
With light, the waters become

laughier.  At the interior of the body
is black
with light organized into what parts?  They say hell is
it intensified.  In what light

cannot do or undergo, excluding
light; that can be stopped or skirted or self-
propogated;  Let's call this
Rays of Light;  lights form as light
formats itself from what was previously

non-light. Does not give us objects but
their shadow, from black to
this scene: indivisible, invisible, to make

the visible seen. In the future
light-
cone of the
event called
past-

light, we will have these
spectra red-shif-
ted (Move
toward me) Who will, blue? (Move
away). Here is my forward, here is my
back. What light says I can't

say The sym-
metry of
light
like stars
at night
versus
stars

in the day. What can we do in dark hours? Abstain?
In the bright we can say

What space, what verge, what amplitude
of the little light like gods' droplets, "rainbow proofs
on the roof"

### Dreamt My Teeth

dreamt my teeth were white as light
I've got a flag on my back; make it be
Not civic, but this meritorious monarch with wings
Of finely woven golden thread just as
The hairs on the human head
Weave a lazy bracelet beneath the rock
When the human is dead

## The Lake

There is light on the geese's
hind parts tonight, my love,
birds who have some care
for their homeland, whuffing
through a lowlit sky with a hinnie view on the country
left behind, yackity yacking
so loud you can probably hear them

where you are, which is far

from the smoky opiatic riches of Arabia, the hinterlands of
Afghanistan illuminated by flying shrapnel
but near to my heart which walks practically beside me

near the yellow leaves, this season's idea
of finery left on low branches, bald treetops like
    monks' pates;

heart leaps like the red berries hanging over the river,
    it's mine
for those in Taliqan who have no view of the Leonids
    tonight

Suspicious geese sound a sudden
alarm & all
the weekend strollers (babies in perambulators)
listen: heads up: YOU are coming home tonight
to put the ripples back in the lake

which is like saying all blackbirds will now be white
and those with "no corner of the earth distant or
    dark enough
to protect them" will rise under rich crimson tents,
    making a virtue of necessity so that
we shall no longer have the desire to have bodies
of substances as incorruptible as crystalline jewels:

        diamond arms, diamond legs, diamond gut
        diamond fingers, diamond hair
        diamond, crystal & diamond heart
        no diamond hands, no diamond lungs
        no heads made of shattering suns

*Summer at St.-Nazaire*

The ordinary rainstorm verves
the sun- or snow-banners

Weather advertises

The sky curdles gradually, brushed
in thin, white cloud-
tissue, a single will scattered

over the errant
multitude

Sand in baggy drifts, in the wombs
of where sand is made, to remain silent
centuries till it is sent

singing into houses; a single grain of sand sets up
house behind a bed or in a shoe, it
relaxes itself and sits
quiet there or

rolls down the coast, back
to sea


Storms express themselves invisibly
in summer, saving up, storms
practice for late September; enter
rains, shot down in avalanche; breezes
break things fragile, bitter


No perfect snow-
banner is ever hung here
in the age of the frozen peoples
The first light of the season throws us
onto the promenade, effulgent, we're remarkable; thaws
    us, shining
into the bottom of the dry
blue
community pool


One train comes up out of the ice, becomes
a sun-
train, the other

goes underground, farther still, where each life
seems to be comparing something
to itself   but it's just forms recognizing the frame
of the human face


..

I do hear
a distinct cheer—is it
the waves, or wind?  I am
really thinking this:
The apples' guts are eaten
Only Argentines are allowed to leave hairs in soap here
Only forests are blue

There are pyrite flecks in the sand and a sandy light falls
    over the sea
We will allow this sea to be blue here, too, but
no green, there is

no green in my country   where machines know
how to turn our bridges upside down when I sit
on a balcony chair and blink, motors
give parties with men
clapping and grinding their teeth. We throw up
sparks like a dentist's drill, even the motors
in cars—what is this fooling?  This

sound of water with wind
in the leaves—quick steps across light—(light jogs
    over water) That boat drags out
the estuary bed, seductive
cables are thrown—Now I know why
the shy men shoulder black hair under the alley
of linden trees: The river is earthly, the cows are
white, the fields, green. The first sounds ever introduced
to earthly life
are standing there, Apaches
crying in the water heater like petits
bourgeois babies. You are the subject
of vertigo? This day? They are doing
an undiscovered something to us sleeping
ones but to those
of us awake sounds are sipped
in plastic cups, taxied out from darker waters.

· ·

The wind fingers everything the wind
can imagine, and there goes
the neighborhood
before they threw down the bombs and said
Your mamma
limb from limb, signifying
more than .44 jive

They are moving things deep
in the depths of the black water; it is not juke
boxes or snapping fingers, not laws
that break
sleeping in caravans or under canvas.


We slept in a trailer. The tattooed father
definitely breathing nearby, it was a star on his right
arm, I believe (truth in arms?), or an electric
skull, maybe a
thunderstorm, pre-military police, half-

gypsy, I don't know anything
he said, about nuclear power (this was my first trip
to Brittany), just
work in it. The wind resumes
its curriculum, a night's resume:  fires on the other side
of the river, cars clearing
throats in the dark.


.. .

Now that they have taken to moving small cities about
    by boat,
using birds for fire works
my city no longer belongs to me, drifting
out to sea,
the grey days of steamships and German missions
The men stand on the promenade and talk amongst them-
    selves   Oh, and
do you think transporting this city was easy?
Wait till we get our orders from headquarters
They'll want us to have the sound of wet car wheels rolling
    over dark roads
Engines gunning in the rain-filled port
Waves described in fire traits: the interlacing
of flames—fluid neighbors on the accidental,
populace sea. This city
is endless with lights. Tomorrow night
I will look and name them all, but tonight

is the pale city where I am chased
through empty, sandy & narrow, anchored streets

The buildings are the color of shells
Fragile, no one lives here. This city is the city

I dreamed: the silent city
of small atoms
with drums in the night
and flag poles snapping, the crinkling of water
going out in muddy runnels

My life here:
                    Coffee in the morning
                            with hot milk
                    After dinner, lots of wine, a cuban cigar, stolen
                            or given, sometimes
                    in the evening, they let me walk on the beach




                        ..

In the old country, the windows
lit up by lightning at night, white, white, like
the ghosts of the Indian braves floating up
in the mist from the river. It was hard
work then burying the dead in eight
foot ditches  A car drives into a voice, voices
rise from the port. I can still hear
the river. In this city, there are
married couples with children. Are they
real?

        Look at these trees
stumbling across a field
of sleeping horses. Water horses, water trees. The water
    castles think
of opossums, stupid
and ugly in their beautiful opossumness, bored
out of their minds.

It's not true that they are not wearing jackets

if god is in each of their sleeves. They have built me
the salt houses of Brittany, salt has made me
a country, Celtic and white. Dame Madame of the
    room and the moon,
creamer and inheritor
of Breton spit in the sea. The way to show someone you
    love him is

to burn time.
I can't stop to not think
              of the necessity
of making plans
right down in the water where the
power is

. .

When I am gone, after I have gone four
into three won't go The garden
goes down to the river, dogs
bark over it; they go to the bad—
Sexological dogs go

barking wild the river
goes down to the sea
Hurry up, hurry little boat, where
do you go, gliding across the skin
of the naked, nighttime estuary in your dark
little suit, bright eyes.  You are making me sick with your
    lagging as if
there were all the time in the world to arrive
in your parts where men in
white T-shirts and shorts wait & women—Well,
what about the women?
In this country, they write
escutcheons for your arrival, especially
flags, colored socks ticking in the wind.

Who is that bird-like figure with big brown eyes and
    black hair
        over your shoulder?


a great heron (if that's what they call it here)
a carved stone up to its neck in the river's knees
Of all these beautiful sides, the bitterest
river ever introduced to earthly life, history shows up
in the smallest notes    I have always had to battle it
with my mouth closed    the little bitch
sliding toward a buoy and break
the ulna, screw back and tilt


the flexible door
    whence I came
                    coaxed
toward further cellulations, a rich
underworld to reflect days, days—they're
    deportable?—condense
about us      "you, your correlative body" sleeping
    next to this native swimmer one
From this point, from the that, a narrative tacks:


There is a husband or wife here, that will change everything

hystic malaria sweating out night in this drawer
White on the pole & white on the horizon You are this
    big: day
falls into a day


White, we are very wet with ourselves
and need a cool place to rest
White, white the ice    White rain & white snow, soon!
    white will be moving
across the river and moving
toward all whiteness erased from the horizon, all blue from
    horizon of green, wrestler
of leaves, a day
falls into a body.




. .

Suddenly, while tying his shoes, Proust
was weighted
down with his grandmother's death. I think you are
wasting time. Are you trying to?
Oh ho! You could at least be arranging
weight, color & shape the way the tide arranges
piles of pink & yellow clams along the beach: It will
mostly not help me. Today, when I returned, I wanted
to turn the table to avoid shadows in my photograph of the
colored glass & shell project. All my
interior goods shut up inside in-
accurately

On the beach—Little wet figures shimmying in sunlight—They
    call these humans.
Hauling the body up
out of sleep, limbs resist air, an indefinite weight—Drag this
stuff up from water, we think

of a small imaginary town somewhere along
the Hudson—& what

does all this thinking & doing do or open?  A knowledge
     of streets,
a collection of rocks, ghost currents. We could see the city

in the early morning sunlight. I can't remember
if they could see us. The morning, the city was a sum
of corridors & we lay in bed & we began
to catalogue the far, far geometry of light,
the claustrophobic ramparts, libraries under the sea,
     exploding
City of Towers. When we think, think

of the rose hour before night & a city
with no people in it to punctuate
streets, T-shirts washed ashore emptied
of human involvement. Time spent in supermarkets searching
     for food,
time spent trying not to eat or smoke or drink
will be over. Two girls running after a soccer ball
on the dock, their legs
in tandem.


•  •

Stars, like a snail's eyes, delicate
    at the stalks
Green stars give glimmery talks
    through dark
        oxygenless air, high
over these hills. A man can enter
a star through the eye's strings

but I came with my blind aunt

in the theoretical year of life
near the leap to invertebrates, circa
    early Detroit

Nudged hematite turned, meteorites
    wiping out smaller cities

where the citizens accept sleep
    without its avenues, sleep's white
arms snaking into the distance and light quietly

over the asphalt. Tentacular sleep

ribbons
into the brain and
quiet now, evening headlights
shine silvery on trucks, a golden

illuminated gull, the arches
of such, hamburgers, but shaking. Peoples, get them

in the grass and rolling
in the dirt so they can

go to heaven. Lest by one false step
you displease the Great
Father.   From now on

no more desire boats,


the cool ash of Ohio at night,
no flammable rivers in *cora deliriums*. Think
of slightly frightened cows,
of girls on rocks,

of the creamy froth spread over
corn—tasseled fields up to the stalks—
a Parrish-blue night runs chilly.

Run, children, run
from water towers with smiley faces
My name is Mightacleia and I come to teach you

the way we are when we are in our houses and doing
the things we know how to do;
constant friction.

When the little boats have alighted on the
surface of the water (their wings
risk to sink
to the bottom
of that sea or lake)

routes stitch up to rivers
    a fortnight tight
        & tourniquet

There is just surface things & depth in these
waters, nothing

in between—to fall
would be to fall, little white
    scratches at the bottom, and trees

too heavy for earth

.  .

Ravines hold out against quiet things, rotting
things move back towards waters we know in the shape
of that sea

There is expertise in any
field of wheat.          You said the word

& a scorpion of dust
& string floated out
of the light & flickered
past our ankles.  Later, the corpse

of a scorpion shriveled
under the door & I
thought I should ask—What's the deal
on scorpions?—& there was a scorpion, hooked &
quiet, a slim
S-shaped wafer—is it
"wildlife"?  Dark, & the bright possible
poison needles its tips in, takes possession

of the mind. There is expertise in any
scorpion, each a series
of surfaces of light exploiting
the laws of vision. Poetry

is not a boxed set, stabbed
with a white arm
of light, no
expertise. Let this

technology (of scorpions) order light, revise
the politics of dogs, and sex,

the dun-colored crepuscular cities out
on the abandoned horizon. Which little piece of dust will
make us happiest? Usk? Usk? Everything I always wanted
    to know

about the 500 kilometers of pipes that run through our city
is coming back to me


. .

*The Bright, the Heavy*

*The skin disappears by a strange enchantment.*

—COMTE DE LAUTRÉAMONT

EVERYTHING IS bright & tender like fish hooks.

Everything is shy, when you pound the muscles, something
   comes out of my eyes.

This is the me in me I used to be able to shake it.

Letting the glove drop.

Watching it fall.

White hands plummeting out of white sleeves. The
   flesh ones.

Here is my hurt kidney.

My hurt foot.

The nervous tic, the one in the lips.

Drawn on the sweet-waist (the super one), here is the fish-
   wife, the shoe-

maker's son on the back

of the donkey's ass.

You can't put a fist through a sleeve if it's a tight one.


I wish I had a bright    a bright

foot, laughing myself into a new mood so much I cry.

THE SIRENS ARE CHASING US over the rooftops with
    the blasts of last snow; Over the
station-tracks like voices screeching along electrical rows.
They are following along just under the wheels; toward the
    sun.
The bright, the heavy one.

(EXCEPT MOSQUITOES, POTATO BUGS, EARWIGS, FLIES, TICKS, LEECHES AND FLEAS)

I just found a paper epithet towards the substantive world.
    Here it is:— Hello? I was
answered in a question: The
World—?/   And how to fix it?/ I don't
have any plans for it and don't see
how to add them to this poem. If you ate your way
    through a peach
would it—?/ I had a dream falling
from the bottom of the pit—/ My relationship
to humans is—?/ Currently my current relationship
is with a human it seems
just fine—/ My favorite thing when I was a child was
animals, and—/ all of them

WE WATCHED
the nature re-runs i.e.

       war; the works of
       love; the eternal
           Each in the end when each

is overthrown I work

the hollow cell who

undo the bands;  dissolve it down now; Now, a second
  whistler enters the train, in
excess; to rend the crossbars at the gates of hate;
  the flaming

rampart at the burning root;  all we wanted was to wander
  the A., held back
by the B.; Now; find strange terms to fit the strangeness
  of the thing: Earth
with eyes & throat full backward thrown

(by words) (we searched to)

unfolded the source; Earth:

THE DOOR TO ACTION ordained me to talk / in the
    growing vapors
about "a body" / about an emblem
to represent / "the body" / the moving parts / of men &
    women /
the body / a dangerous thing / between the wrong hands
(of cancer) / In the village, everything was measured
from this center: "two fingers wide"/
that one washes ones hands/ before dinner/ so the bread/
goes in clean/

THEY TORE OFF my adolescent shoulder
ripped out the muscles one-by-one

from so far away I make
my memory come back

kick-the-can, capture-the-flag, Marco/

                                       Polo

in the muddy labyrinths, the drifting
body — drift

down to earth now
with the impulse of a hand to raise

or fall; make follow the body

pressing the ground with such weight: a foot
engaged with weight

the soaped water has seen  /  risen
& fallen  /  entire  /  generations  /  spilled on earth
despite the efforts  /  of the surface  /  of a body

let drop / the lantern / torch / of hate / the rag
try these legs     doing this: walk

CITIZEN, THERE ARE TERRESTRIAL complications resulting
    from the fury with which one puts
one's metacarpals into action, the articulate mis-
    firings; possibilities

of hypothetical error where I place my legs
in the horizontal direction to re-

light a match as if it had several
points of ignition, thus

Do I know the rose of clouds?
The faucet's works and waters declaring themselves
rivulets?

What blood comes to promenade its redness, the blood
of a person shouldn't leave so

easily slipped between the sleeve, sleeped
beneath the shoulders of the bull, The blade

adheres to the body—no one can extract it—Should we

open the throat or place on the heart a delirious note—

I interrogate it less for the majesty of its form than
    for its table of reality  The Heart
is sobriety-driving  The Heart

INCLINE the binary brain toward it (earth) and hear
the astonishing song of rocks & dirt — Who walks
    here over
crusts formed before fishes or wings — all the
first things built and ten million more made on the surface
between then  and /  — : what next?  with:  what's
last?  a blank made of
anti-matter I can't
eat — identical sheep


        Tell them
there is only
a fever that dresses me
in each pure animal

        Tell them
my parents were the math of the
world in a dream taking place autochthonically



SCENE:

We fish for small halibut at the bottom of a man-made lake.

A tender, living fish uncurls its meat. But in dropping the line we trigger the lake-motors and treadle-blades shred it—a fault in the memory or in the machinery. Bits of flesh suspended in the bottom-water where light has a pale voice, milk-jammed,—easy-torn fish

Please Welcome, Rise, tight packed atoms of flesh

I.

I KNEW A GIRL who was trying to learn how to make herself cry. There are several methods:

1. You think of waters in a body. (Each liquid has its proper level.) When you are sick in the kidneys, your liquids are wrong, water comes out of your eyes.

2. You think of something red.

3. You cry.

II.

Yesterday was an orange bottle, crushed apricots over a field, baby aspirin. Baby aspirin is orange, you might remember this.

The day before: a vast expanse of sponge cake laid out over a curving glass surface. They wanted me to eat.

Last summer I saw red; this began around the edges of June.

When we think of red, we think of emotional red. We think of the fervent body of red. Red corpuscles, redtips, red winged, a blackbird. A wire attachment to the heart that connects to an amp helps us remember a red thing that lives in the body and makes noise.

When I used to think, I used to think in blue or green.

Now that I have thought in red and orange, I think I am acquiring colors. I think a new orange thing will appear tomorrow.

In a dream, I dreamed a red strawberry tree.

I TOOK off my dress & out fell my bones

—

My dress is crumbling

—

This, finally, is a record of my life.

ONE DAY, THIS happens:

My head is full of snow.

Quiet is on my head.

The ice-man keeps hitting me over the head
with an ice-bar hard as ice;

I fall down; I get up; the ice-man
hits me on the head again.

I see this happen:
It happens again. I get

up again, the in-
explicable will.

Silence is on my head  he breaks it
in the lung-hunt (air);

tympan-crack under the shock
of air-mass sonore;  he unties

the insides of my ear

toward the clean sound, the loud sound
the cotton then and iron sound in snow;

at the indicating post, arrowing the good
hypothesis:  Don't try to make me

know the soul-
envelope over

the grid of language:  a microscopic
futility.  Here:  silence

is on my head it's
growing in my head I

dreamed it there bigger
in the ice-sphere he breaks it Come

break it What

can guarantee me

from the cold

LAST NIGHT I ATE A HUMAN in a dream——or at least its
   bones——I thought
that fingers might split over the touch of human
skin  That day on the subway we heard the buzzing of the
   mechanic's wing like
ice cubes rattling against each other——

Tuesday:  snow in the grates

Torn into the quick, it's small things
that become difficult, buying apples
not pears, placing the fingers inside the holes——

Now I am this living instrument

of a heart, two hands, etc., given loose to animal
luminosity & fabulous humors. These, too, do grow
out of (me) (a) the (very) body of all surprise——

I SAID to them then in their sleeps
Your sheets have wandered off.
Let them, he said, let them.

THIS spectacle:  the movie-house universe

moving.  Hold still. — to touch this you with a twelve-
fingered attention, concentrated
on the flesh, made by

      the laws of science

      Out of an eye I made
a long tear

a diamond-string system of color—, & in the evening
out in space you see sixteen sunsets come & go

in one day from brilliant
red to deepest
              blue—& the lights
   "over
the pole-bathing seas"—


Settle down now, bring them (here)
near a center, an axis, for

what ration of relief in the world
(to be found) (inside)

("a body") "the exact point[s] I inhabit" ("on earth")

FROM THE FROTHIEST RIVERS on the rockiest globe,
   escutcheon me
with a signing coat far east of us, my insignias arms is missing
something in the night-restaurant I swallow

the pit's full-middle
from an endometrium dark I did could

build a new grill   a new grrr    new girrl

In this ejecta process, known visitors
from other planets are a small fraction
of alien troves lying undiscovered here
on Earth, mainly mistaken for rocks.


HERE IS THE MAN WHO GOT HIS GOLD eye put out
   (7 x 4 foot frame)—What was he doing
so close to the ground?


Now he's a dark, with wrinkles and crow's feet       his
   eye was a rock
in the system [sissies] that relegated animals to childhood
   and put


brakes
at the bottom of the beast


Like him, they have risen
so that they no longer exist on earth


What do they do with the missing parts?  [[(Cars, or
   all that is left of the picture
      is two big toes)]]

Thinking with things
as they exist (ruins) the mind tries
to rebuild (de-composed) feet.

There were days when objects came to me easily
(a coat, a tire) Knowing or not the value of matter, it's easy

      to lose

              three inches in a lifetime   (bits of
                    moon  blasted loose at dawn)

skewed by the tug of other planets, I might form a ring
that rotates    near Jupiter    (shed skin)   a piece of
   debris from Venus
              moves  to fall
to Earth, bits
of life push
between borders—kiss kiss this
Parthenon dust

It doesn't take that much walking

to make a path through the grass but the dandelion
   is poisonous

Now they grow artichokes on top of the church
For the melting lamb, the snow-or-sun-daughter they eat in
   April, it's what

the crowned heart told
about the "candleblows" of sunlight—

I saw those columns from the bathroom window—
that stone even my hand could smash




As the meat was created
to hang on the hours of earth

at the backside of the peacock, where the eyes are spread
is the original anti-matter, the Achilles heel

so according to the inscription on the votive thighs, Love
is of antidiluvian, has

tender feet, steps
on the heads of men

Love, what is Love love of


We are currently standing in North

(Somewhere in the Western Ocean we will live for love)

(Love, come) (within) (the long range) (of age)


carrying a scratch back from the Acropolis
with a gesture of epiphany toward the right hand
Like the man who forgot then re-learned his language

word-by-word. Each day, in his language I learn a new word
A new word comes back to me— μιδέν (zero), κουκάλι
     (spoon)

CUTTING UP its contents, this apartment is a scene
obtained from tapering blanket-pieces
when stripped &  hoisted

First comes white-horse
Then the receptacle piece
honed from 1,000 nameless emergencies woven within
     the hour


By the ordinary laws of anatomy,

I, too, was given a heart. They could have hidden
something in there, in the beginning, without us knowing: A
     bottle cap,
a bit of plastic.  Such as

the oyster, I'll get over it. And when they opened the chest
each night sets fire to its own ear     eye   throat, heart

THE PANIC ALPHABET—in water-voice packets—a longitudinal breaking—the provisions of sang-froid that I collect—half of ordinary breathing—I apostrophe the hot place—feverish whistle—annhiliate the laws of physical—when my feet fool the sidewalk rock—into nocturnal happiness why

do you shine so?

(THE MACHINE OF BEING, OR, DRAWING TO BE
LOOKED AT ASKEW)


One day, tired of heeling the path
abrupt I will

stop

and melt the nerves of thought
in my hard head, sieved

in the magic pavement. The flying fishes of this brainy
    instrument
are accorded

as pearled notes
are cramping across

the atmosphere's elastic bands.
What have my friends given me?

What have I given them?
Stranded in the blood or the book—impossible

globes & strapped an impassible task
I imitate stars. What have I dreamed of

the most grandiose?

DISAPPEARING by the arch—of his foot—an access of loam—the terrestrial complications—of a hole or—an unknown stone—*un cortège de rayons*—abandon this stain—the Annals of blue—Apply my 400 spirit-things—under his armpit—& make him grow—& gain the large—to easililess kiss the circumference—of a planet—

in the seat of this neck
change Orphan to Orphic

in the leaves of my book of my bed *je me trouve tres trist-an Tzara*; change
BALZAC to PROZAC; take it

with a grain of strange
Eurosugar, let it be you

to change marine to Maine, conjugate
drunk pockets in matter's conjugal foyer

HORIZON-COUCH / QUIET DOWN / that night
has covered / my steps /

numb larvae / fuck the dress / of dumb / humanity /
reefs / of other / chalk /

night is not / completely / arrived here /
arranged over / the stunned world /

in the foyer / I have a plan to report
to the orbicular planets / a system

of light revolt / Now enter
the coat / of-gold / of-good

the ballad of remorse / will no longer /
be played here / now green the eyes / away
from the walls of bite / precipitating the blind-course
toward the crown / of cliffs / simple

vapors of combustion / the career-fire / will
    sequester itself

(WE WORK BY THE MOUTH or by the yard)


Bodyings          sudden-stunned
studded in        non-bound

So far gone       have I gone
in the            which side
throttling joy    now yield me
my pillow         the theoretic
bright one;       light (of heaven)
heated by         earth's heat (let it)
empty in          to my living
foot              advanced on this;
unheed            night-damp on the clothes
that dark         had wet (now dry)
gliding           strangeness to strange to
invest            the thin;

I stand in this air's full middle—

the lean-shade siding
the solid rib

PROPPED UP on—two feet—which act under orders—
tendons overspreading—thoughts—flown out the body—
See—the truck—running down hills—this—natural
home—(in the stars)—See your eyes—grown full—out of
derelict blue—

## *Dream Poem Two (reprisal)*

dreamt our city was destroyed, and we were there
while the huge, bullet-shaped bombs
whistled and smashed into buildings,
lights crashing around & above
us; dark, night-time sky;
the end of our days in
cafés, in beds, in each
others' arms, in safety,
in dark or in light in libraries,
in markets with bright things all
around; the only thing left
in the dream is to make love

in a light-filled gutter; so let
Odysseus's foot fall
back in the basin tonight, the bright

beads of water
bathed in blonde air

GREEN INTEGER
Pataphysics and Pedantry

Douglas Messerli, *Publisher*

Essays, Manifestos, Statements, Speeches, Maxims,
Epistles, Diaristic Notes, Narratives, Natural Histories,
Poems, Plays, Performances, Ramblings, Revelations
and all such ephemera as may appear necessary
to bring society into a slight tremolo of confusion
and fright at least.

\*

Green Integer Books